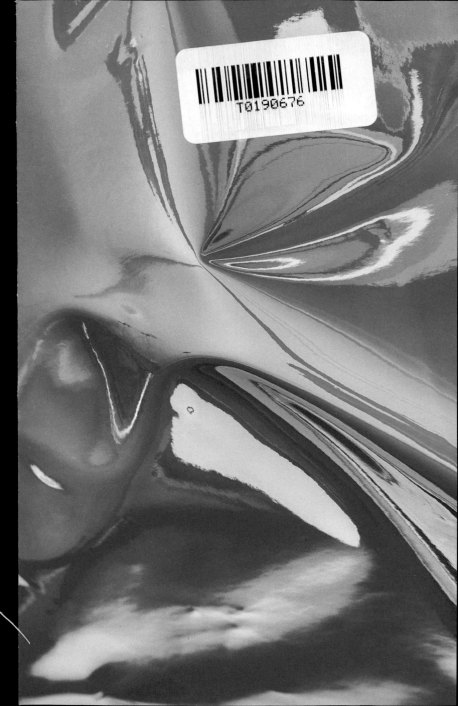

DISCO
COCKTAILS

DISCO
COCKTAILS

MORE THAN 50 CLASSIC & KITSCH DRINKS FROM THE 70S & 80S

RYLAND PETERS & SMALL
LONDON • NEW YORK

DAVID T. SMITH
& KELI RIVERS

photography by
Timothy Atkins

To the pilots of the airwaves and tornadoes of the turntables: J-Dog, JVS, Paul Miller and Johnnie Walker.

For Diamond Ken and our shared belief in the magic of disco beats and properly made Corpse Revivers.

Senior designer Toni Kay
Production manager Gordana Simakovic
Creative director Leslie Harrington
Editorial director Julia Charles

Food stylist Lorna Brash
Prop stylist Luis Peral
Indexer Hilary Bird

First published in 2024 by Ryland Peters & Small
20–21 Jockey's Fields
London WC1R 4BW
and
341 E 116th Street
New York, 10029

www.rylandpeters.com

10 9 8 7 6 5 4 3 2 1

Text © David T. Smith & Keli Rivers 2024.
Design and photography © Ryland Peters & Small 2024.

ISBN: 978-1-78879-640-8

A CIP record for this book is available from the British Library.
US Library of Congress CIP data has been applied for.

Printed in China

MIX
Paper | Supporting responsible forestry
FSC® C008047

CONTENTS

INTRODUCTION

Disco cocktails are all about being fun, fruity (in some sense or another), fluorescent and flamboyant. In a decade where the world seemed to be falling apart, people escaped with great music, fantastic parties, and cocktails to elevate their mood.

Liqueurs that were particularly popular during the time period were blue Curaçao, an orange liqueur made with Curaçao oranges and dyed a startling shade of azure (green and orange versions are also available, but far less popular) and the luminescent green Midori. Midori, a Japanese melon liqueur, was originally called 'Hermes Melon Liqueur' when it launched in 1964. In 1978, it relaunched at New York's world famous nightclub Studio 54 with the cast and crew of the movie *Saturday Night Fever* in attendance – how much more disco can you get?

Today, there has never been a wider range of ingredients – both in quality and availability – that can be used to reimagine these cocktails, allowing them to be enjoyed more easily by people around the world. In many ways, these drinks have never tasted so good and yet lost nothing of their colourfully kitsch appeal!

This book is divided into chapters: Classic and Contemporary focus on drinks that were either invented or popularized in the 1970s and '80s, along with some modern variations. The Experimental chapter goes a bit wild, inspired by the spirit of soul, funk and disco. Finally, the Seasonal section gives you a vibrant themed cocktail, perfect for year-round enjoyment.

TOP TIPS AND HELPFUL HINTS

VEGAN /DAIRY-FREE ALTERNATIVES

Egg white: this is typically added to cocktails to produce a silky texture and add a little frothy crema to the top; these vegan alternatives can replicate that effect when necessary. There are multiple substitutes that you can try, such as 'Oggs', 'Just Eggs' or the water from a can of chickpeas (aquafaba).

Egg liqueurs: In place of Advocaat or VOV Egg Liqueur: Take 100 ml/3½ fl oz. of ready-made vegan custard or créme Anglaise and 35 ml/2 generous tablespoons of brandy in a jug/pitcher and mix thoroughly with a whisk until smooth. Use as instructed.

Cream: There are a number of different non-dairy creams that can be used, depending on what's available in your region. For this book, Elmlea 100% Plant Double was used to test the recipes; any kind of vegan thick or whipping cream is ideal.

GARNISHES

Rimming glasses: A number of the recipes in this book use glasses with coloured sugar, salt or cookie crumbs on the rims. Whilst citrus juice can be used to stick the sugar to the glass, it will be held in place more firmly with beaten egg white. Place the beaten egg white on a plate, dip the rim of your glass in it, then in your coloured sugar (or salt). Place the glass in your fridge or freezer until ready to use.

Coloured sugar/salt: Add sugar/salt into an electric mixer and add one drop of food grade food colouring at a time, mixing on low until the desired colour is obtained. Be warned, however: too much colour can stain your lips and/or teeth!

Cherries: There are many fancy (and delicious!) gourmet cocktail cherries available, but most of their recipes have been designed to feature the striking bright (almost neon) red Maraschino cherries to add a visual spectacle to drinks. Example brands include Opies or Filthy. Ultimately, the choice is yours.

TECHNIQUE

Dry shaking: Shaking a cocktail without ice first, is a technique most commonly used to emulsify egg whites into your cocktail, creating a more unified mouthfeel. First, add all of the ingredients (except any that are carbonated) into your shaker along with the egg white and shake well for 1–2 minutes. Then add ice and follow the remaining instructions in the cocktail recipe.

CLASSIC

THE MIDORI SOUR

FRUIT, FUN AND FLUORESCENT, THE MIDORI SOUR IS THE PERFECT WAY TO KICK OFF A NIGHT OF BOOGIEING.

50 ml/1¾ oz. Midori
25 ml/¾ oz. lemon juice
1 egg white
5–10 ml/¼ –⅓ oz. sparkling/
   soda water (optional)
melon slice and lemon peel
   twist, to garnish

SERVES 1

Add the ingredients (except the soda) to a shaker and dry shake vigorously. Add ice and shake again, before fine-straining into an ice-filled rocks glass. Top-up with sparkling water, if liked, garnish with a melon slice and a twist of lemon peel and serve.

Variation: For a more sour drink, use equal parts (25 ml/¾ oz. each) of vodka, Midori and lemon juice.

THE JAPANESE SLIPPER

THIS FRUITY COCKTAIL IS A MUST-TRY FOR FANS OF SOUR CANDY, SUCH AS SOUR PATCH KIDS OR HARIBO TANGFASTICS.

25 ml/¾ oz. Midori
25 ml/¾ oz. orange liqueur,
   such as Cointreau
25 ml/¾ oz. lemon juice
cocktail cherry, to garnish

SERVES 1

Shake the ingredients vigorously with ice and then fine-strain into a V-shaped cocktail glass. Garnish with a cocktail cherry and serve.

HARVEY WALLBANGER

THE HARVEY WALLBANGER STARTED OUT LIFE AS THE
SCREWDRIVER (VODKA AND ORANGE JUICE) BEFORE
GALLIANO, AN ITALIAN VANILLA AND SPICE LIQUEUR,
WAS ADDED. SOME EARLY RECIPES EVEN CALL THE DRINK
THE 'ITALIAN SCREWDRIVER'. THE SLIGHTLY FRAZZLED
SURFER CHARACTER OF THE SAME NAME WAS CREATED
ESPECIALLY FOR GALLIANO'S AMERICAN DISTRIBUTOR.

35 ml/1¼ oz. vodka

100 ml/3½ oz. orange juice
(ideally freshly squeezed)

15 ml/½ oz. Galliano L'Autentico
(in a pinch, the vanilla version works, too)

orange peel twist or orange slice, to garnish

SERVES 1

Add the vodka and then the orange juice to
a tall, ice-filled glass and stir. Pour the Galliano
on the top. Add a twist of orange peel or orange
slice to garnish plus a straw or stirrer and serve.

Variations: Adding sloe gin and Southern
Comfort to the above recipe creates a Sloe
Comfortable Screw Against the Wall: a more
intense drink with a touch of fruitiness. Another
variation involves replacing the Galliano with
triple sec, creating a Sloe Comfortable Screw
Between the Sheets, which is full of honey,
citrus and spice notes.

WISCONSIN OLD FASHIONED

MANY WILL BE FAMILIAR WITH THE OLD FASHIONED, BUT THE DAIRY STATE HAS ITS OWN VERSION. THE MAIN DIFFERENCE IS THAT IT IS FRUITIER AND MADE WITH BRANDY – IDEALLY A DOMESTIC US BRANDY, SUCH AS KORBEL OR LAIRD'S APPLEJACK. FOR THOSE OF A EUROPEAN PERSUASION, GERMANY'S ASBACH OR ITALY'S VECCHIA ROMAGNA WORK WELL.

1 cocktail cherry

1 orange wedge

1 teaspoon brown sugar

3–4 dashes Angostura Bitters

50 ml/1¾ oz. brandy

SERVES 1

Muddle the first four ingredients directly in the glass until the sugar has largely dissolved. Add the brandy and some ice (this can be small cubes or even crushed ice). Stir with a stirrer that is left in the glass, and serve

Variations: For a sweet version, top up with sparkling lemon-lime soda (e.g. 7Up or Sprite); for a sour version, add sparkling/soda water and a squeeze of lemon and lime; and for a press, add a 50:50 mix of ginger ale and sparkling water.

NEW YORK SOUR

THE NEW YORK SOUR, AKA THE CONTINENTAL SOUR OR SOUTHERN WHISKEY SOUR, DATES BACK TO THE 1880S AND IS ESSENTIALLY A WHISKEY SOUR WITH A FLOAT OF RED WINE ON THE TOP, WHICH ADDS A VISUAL SPECTACLE.

60 ml/2 oz. bourbon
25 ml/³⁄₄ oz. simple/sugar syrup
30 ml/1 oz. lemon juice
15 ml/¹⁄₂ oz. egg white or suitable substitute
5–10 ml/¹⁄₄ –¹⁄₃ oz. red wine

SERVES 1

Add the ingredients (except the wine) to a shaker and dry shake. Add ice and shake again, vigorously. Fine-strain into an ice-filled tumbler and layer the red wine on top by gently pouring it over the back of a barspoon.

Note: The choice of wine here makes a difference and it's not worth scrimping on. If you've having a nice bottle of red with a meal at home, you can sacrifice a splash for a pre-dinner aperitif! Malbec works particularly well, giving the drink a slight raspberry-ripple quality.

MANHATTAN SKYLINE

NAMED AFTER DAVID SHIRE'S FUNKY INSTRUMENTAL TRACK FROM SATURDAY NIGHT FEVER, THIS IS A PLAYFUL TWIST ON THE MANHATTAN, SERVED ON THE ROCKS.

50 ml/1³⁄₄ oz. rye whiskey
25 ml/³⁄₄ oz. red vermouth
10 ml/¹⁄₃ oz. maraschino
3–4 dashes orange bitters
5–10 ml/¹⁄₄ –¹⁄₃ oz. red wine
orange peel twist, to garnish

SERVES 1

Add the ingredients (except the wine) to an ice-filled mixing glass and stir. Pour into an ice-filled rocks glass and float the wine on top by gently pouring it over the back of a barspoon. Garnish with an orange peel twist and serve.

BLOODY MARY

INVENTED AT HARRY'S NEW YORK BAR IN PARIS, THIS IS THE GO-TO BRUNCH COCKTAIL.

50 ml/1¾ oz. vodka

150 ml/5 oz. tomato juice
(ideally plain and unseasoned)

seasonings to your taste (e.g. salt, black pepper,
Worcestershire sauce, celery salt and Tabasco)

lemon wedge, stuffed olive on a pick and
celery stick/stalk, to garnish

SERVES 1

Add the ingredients to a tall, ice-filled glass, stir and season to taste, and stir again. Add the garnish and serve with a celery stick or other stirrer.

Note: It's easy for a Bloody Mary virgin to go overboard on the seasonings, resulting in an undrinkable mess that puts them off for life. If in doubt, just try a little black pepper.

Variations: If you're not a fan of vodka, you can also switch out the base spirit: using gin instead creates a Red Snapper; blanco tequila creates a Bloody Maria; and white whiskey creates a Bloody Millie.

UMARTINI

The Umartini ('oo-martini') is a fun umami chaser to your Bloody Mary. Rinse a small martini glass (a shot glass will do in a pinch) with 2–3 drops Worcestershire sauce, add 25 ml/¾ oz. either vodka or gin (straight from the freezer) and enjoy!

BLUE LAGOON

THIS COCKTAIL WAS INVENTED IN THE 1960S BY ANDREW
MACELHONE OF HARRY'S NEW YORK BAR IN PARIS. ACCORDING
TO BRÉVIAIRE DE L'AMOUR SORCIER (1969), THE DRINK WAS
ORIGINALLY SERVED IN A BOWL FOR TWO PEOPLE WITH
CRUSHED ICE, CANDIED FRUITS AND TWO STRAWS. HERE'S
A MODERN-DAY RECIPE FOR ONE.

50 ml/1¾ oz.vodka
25 ml/¾ oz. blue Curaçao
10 ml/⅓ oz. lime juice or lime cordial
120 ml/4 oz. lemonade/lemon soda
cocktail cherry and orange slice, to garnish

SERVES 1

Add the vodka to a tall, ice-filled glass, followed
by the blue Curaçao and lime juice. Top up with
lemonade, garnish with a cocktail cherry and an
orange slice and serve.

MEDITERRANEAN
Replacing the vodka with gin and garnishing
with a long, thin piece of lemon peel creates a
Mediterranean – the garnish is as long as the name!

DIABLO AZULITO
A Diablo Azulito uses blanco tequila as the base
ingredient, ginger beer as the soda mixer, and
a splash of lime juice, not cordial.

DISCO DUCK
The Disco Duck uses unaged rum and a lemon peel
garnish, with some mini chocolate eggs on the side.

TEQUILA SUNRISE

THE ORIGINS OF A COMBINATION OF TEQUILA, SODA WATER, LIME, AND LIQUEUR GO BACK TO THE 1930S AND THE BILTMORE HOTEL, ARIZONA. THE MODERN, SIMPLIFIED VERSION OF THIS COCKTAIL WAS INVENTED IN 1972 AT THE TRIDENT BAR IN SAUSALITO, CALIFORNIA. THE ROLLING STONES HAD A PARTY THERE TO KICK OFF THEIR US TOUR AND BECAME FANS OF THE DRINK. IN 1973, THE EAGLES NAMED A SONG AFTER IT ON THEIR *DESPERADO* ALBUM.

45 ml/1½ oz. tequila
90 ml/3 oz. orange juice (ideally freshly squeezed)
15 ml/½ oz. grenadine
cocktail cherry, orange slice and mint sprig, to garnish

SERVES 1

Add the tequila and orange juice to a tall ice-filled glass and stir. Slowly pour the grenadine down the inside of the glass to create a 'sink': this causes the bottom of the drink to be red and for the colour to bleed up into the juice, creating a 'sunrise' effect.

Note: A blanco tequila gives the drink a bright crispness – perfect for the first drink of the evening – whilst a reposado adds a more spiced, woody warmth, fitting for the later hours.

TEQUILA SUNSET

A Tequila Sunset replaces the orange juice with grapefruit or ruby grapefruit juice. The former can be a little bitter, but the ruby grapefruit adds a lovely, soft fruitiness and a delightful pink glow to the drink.

CONTEMPORARY

DISCO MARTINIS

**FUN, SWEET AND COLOURFUL WITH A NOD TO THE EXOTIC.
BE CAREFUL NOT TO SPILL THESE ON THE DANCEFLOOR!**

LYCHEE MARTINI

50 ml/1¾ oz. vodka
30 ml/1 oz. lychee syrup (from a can)
10 ml/⅓ oz. bianco vermouth
lychees, to garnish

SERVES 1

Vigorously shake the
ingredients with ice and
fine-strain into a cocktail
glass. Garnish with a few
lychees on a pick and serve.

KEY LIME MARTINI

ginger cookie crumbs, to rim
the glass
45 ml/1½ oz. vanilla vodka
20 ml/⅔ oz. Malibu
15 ml/½ oz. lime juice
15 ml/½ oz. pineapple juice
15 ml/½ oz. double/heavy cream
10 ml/⅓ oz. simple/sugar syrup
lime slice, to garnish

SERVES 1

Rim the glass with crumbs. Shake
the ingredients with ice and
fine-strain into the glass. Garnish
with a lime slice and serve.

CABLE CAR MARTINI

cinnamon and sugar, to rim the glass
50 ml/1¾ oz. spiced rum
25 ml/¾ oz. orange liqueur
25 ml/¾ oz. lemon juice
10 ml/⅓ oz. simple/sugar syrup
orange zest twist, to garnish

SERVES 1

Rim a martini glass
with sugar and
cinnamon. Shake
the ingredients with
ice, then fine-strain
into the glass.
Garnish with a twist
of orange zest
and serve.

AMARETTO SOUR

AMARETTO IS AN ITALIAN ALMOND LIQUEUR THAT COMES IN TWO MAIN TYPES: ONE TASTES LIKE SWEET ALMOND OR MARZIPAN (E.G. DISARONNO), WHILST THE OTHER IS FLAVOURED WITH AMARETTI COOKIES (E.G. LAZZARONI). EITHER WAY, THIS DRINK IS A FAB WAY TO ENJOY THEM.

50 ml/1¾ oz. amaretto
25 ml/¾ oz. lemon juice
15 ml/½ oz. egg white (or suitable substitute)
lemon peel twist, to garnish

SERVES 1

Dry shake the ingredients to create the foam, then shake again with ice. Strain into an ice-filled tumbler and serve.

THE IMPROVED AMARETTO SOUR

45 ml/1½ oz. amaretto
30 ml/1 oz. applejack, apple brandy or bourbon
30 ml/1 oz. lemon juice
15 ml/½ oz. simple/sugar syrup
15 ml/½ oz. egg white (or suitable substitute)
apple fan, to garnish

SERVES 1

Prepare as the above recipe. This variation offers juicy, fruity apple flavours with a combination of sweet and tart notes, followed by a hint of nutty smoke. Using bourbon adds some woody maple and brown sugar that complements the amaretto.

PIÑA COLADA

A SUN-KISSED COMBO OF RUM, PINEAPPLE AND COCONUT, THOUGHT TO HAVE ORIGINATED FROM 1950S PUERTO RICO.

30 ml/1 oz. white rum, such as Bacardi

30 ml/1 oz. coconut cream

90 ml/3 oz. pineapple juice

pineapple wedge (and leaf) and cocktail cherry, to garnish

SERVES 1

Shake all of the ingredients vigorously with ice. Fine-strain into an ice-filled glass and garnish with a wedge of pineapple, a cherry and – ideally – a bit of cocktail frivolity, such as an umbrella or fun stirrer.

Variation: Alternatively, you can blend the ingredients with ice to a smoothie-like consistency. You might want to add a little more rum (20–30 ml/⅔–1 oz.) and maybe even a scoop of vanilla ice cream.

CHAMPAGNE COLADA

For extra effervescent extravagance, add 20–30 ml/⅔–1 oz. sparkling wine to the final drink.

BLUE HAWAIIAN

Add 15–20 ml/½–⅔ oz. blue Curaçao to the above recipe. It changes the drink by adding a distinctive blue hue and an additional kiss of citrus flavour.

SMOKY PIÑA

Add 15 ml/½ oz. smoky whisky, such as Lagavulin or Laphroaig; the peat works very well with the fruity pineapple juice.

SEX ON THE BEACH

IS THIS ONE OF THE MOST CYNICAL (ALBEIT TASTY) COCKTAILS IN HISTORY? IT WAS CREATED IN 1980S FLORIDA BY TED PIZIO TO HELP HIM WIN THE CHALLENGE OF SELLING THE MOST PEACH SCHNAPPS. THE TERMS 'SEX' AND 'BEACH' WERE INCLUDED TO APPEAL TO SPRING BREAK VACATIONERS.

50 ml/1¾ oz. vodka
25 ml/¾ oz. peach schnapps
50 ml/1¾ oz. cranberry juice
50 ml/1¾ oz. orange juice
sprig of redcurrants and orange slice,
    to garnish

SERVES 1

Add the ingredients to an ice-filled glass and gently stir with a straw. Serve with the straw and a colourful fruit garnish, such as redcurrants and an orange slice.

WOO WOO
Make the above recipe with double the cranberry juice, but no orange juice.

AFTERNOON DELIGHT
Replace the vodka with bourbon and the peach schnapps with Southern Comfort.

SEX ON THE DRIVEWAY
Replace the fruit juices with 15 ml/½ oz. blue curaçao, 100 ml/3½ oz. sparkling lemonade/lemon soda, and a squeeze of lemon juice.

JELLO SHOTS

MIXING ALCOHOL AND GELATIN HAS A HISTORY STRETCHING
BACK MORE THAN 700 YEARS, WHEN MEAT JELLY WAS MIXED
WITH WINE. HAPPILY THE MORE PALATABLE VARIATION
STARTED IN THE 1950S AND JELLO SHOTS HAVE BEEN
A COLOURFUL STAPLE OF PARTIES EVER SINCE.

12 cubes jelly/jello
280 ml/10 oz. boiling water
140 ml/5 oz. cold water
140 ml/5 oz. spirit of choice

MAKES 16

Chop the jelly/jello up into small pieces, add the
boiling water, and stir until they have dissolved. Add
the cold water and spirit and stir. Pour the mix into
shot glasses and place into a refrigerator to set.
Serve on a tray, cold from the fridge.

Variations: There is such a wide range of jelly/Jello
available that the combination of flavours and spirits
is only limited to your imagination, but here are some
examples. When using gin, a more nuanced flavour
profile tends to get lost, so it's best to use a punchy
gin such as Thunderflower Navy Strength.

Lime jelly: *vodka, white rum, blanco Tequila*
Lemon jelly: *vodka, gin, Pisco*
Blackcurrant jelly: *vodka, Scotch whisky*
Orange jelly: *vodka, gin*
Strawberry jelly: *vodka, gin*
Raspberry jelly: *vodka, gin*
Peach jelly: *vodka, bourbon*

PISCO SOUR

PISCO IS A GRAPE-BASED SPIRIT FROM SOUTH AMERICA, MADE IN BOTH PERU AND CHILE. PERUVIAN PISCO IS BOTTLED STRAIGHT FROM THE STILL, WHILST CHILEAN PISCO CAN BE DISTILLED MULTIPLE TIMES. THIS OFTEN MEANS THE PISCO FROM PERU HAS MORE CHARACTER.

50 ml/1¾ oz. pisco

25 ml/¾ oz. lemon juice

25 ml/¾ oz. simple/sugar syrup

15 ml/½ oz. egg white (or suitable substitute)

3-4 drops Amargo Chuncho bitters or other aromatic bitters, to finish

edible flower, to garnish (optional)

SERVES 1

Dry shake the ingredients before adding ice and shaking again vigorously. Fine-strain into a coupe glass, add a few drops of bitters to the top and garnish with an edible flower to serve, if liked.

Variations: For limitless variations, you can substitute the sugar syrup for the liqueur of your choice. This will create a slightly dryer drink, so you might want to still add 10 ml/⅓ oz. sugar syrup alongside the liqueur. Each liqueur will give a different character: Midori is rich and fruity; Galliano is sweet and creamy; and blue Curaçao adds a citrus vibrancy (both in flavour and colour). You can even substitute Campari for a drink that is bracing, bitter and tart.

HURRICANE

THE HURRICANE COCKTAIL DATES BACK TO PAT O'BRIEN'S BAR
IN NEW ORLEANS IN THE LATE 1930S. LEGEND HAS THAT IT WAS
MADE WITH RUM BECAUSE OF THE LIMITED SUPPLY OF WHISKY.
THERE ARE MANY DIFFERENT VARIATIONS ON THE RECIPE,
WITH SOME INCLUDING A LONG-LOST TIKI SYRUP KNOWN AS
FASSIONOLA. THE FOLLOWING RECIPE IS DESIGNED TO BE
AS ACCESSIBLE AS POSSIBLE.

25 ml/³⁄₄ oz. dark rum (see Note, below)

25 ml/³⁄₄ oz. white rum

25 ml/³⁄₄ oz. Passoa passion fruit liqueur
or 15 ml/¹⁄₂ oz. passion fruit syrup/purée

50 ml/1³⁄₄ oz. orange juice

50 ml/1³⁄₄ oz. pineapple juice

20 ml/²⁄₃ oz. lime juice

2–3 dashes Angostura Bitters

orange and lime slices, to garnish

SERVES 1

Shake all the ingredients vigorously with ice and
fine-strain into an ice-filled glass. Garnish with
orange and lime slices and serve.

Note: Despite its fruity nature, the choice of rums
does make a big difference to this drink. For the
dark rum, a Jamaican pot still such as Smith & Cross,
with its sweet, fruity esters and grassiness, makes
a rockin' choice.

GODFATHER

THE GODFATHER AND ITS VARIATIONS ALL HAVE NAMES INSPIRED BY THE NEO-NOIR CINEMA OF THE 1970S.

50 ml/1¾ oz. Scotch whisky
   (25 ml/¾ oz. for the sweeter original version)
25 ml/¾ oz. amaretto
strip of orange peel, to garnish

SERVES 1

Add the ingredients to an ice-filled tumbler and gently stir. Garnish with a strip of orange peel and serve.

Note: The sweeter original version, with a 2:1 ratio of whisky to amaretto, produces a delightful drink to sip all evening. The 50:50 version is rich and sweet and works as an after dinner cocktail to serve in place of dessert.

BRONSON
Use bourbon instead of Scotch for a simply delightful variation named after the actor Charles Bronson.

FRENCH CONNECTION
Using brandy instead of Scotch, makes a French Connection, which is rich with flavours of raisins.

MAGNUM FORCE
Use Calvados or applejack instead of Scotch to add crisp, fresh flavours and a gentle nuttiness.

EXPERIMENTAL

BLAME IT ON THE BOOGIE

A RIFF ON THE LONG ISLAND ICED TEA, COLOURFUL AND FRUITY!

10 ml/⅓ oz. blue Curaçao
15 ml/½ oz. vodka
15 ml/½ oz. blanco tequila
15 ml/½ oz. white rum
15 ml/½ oz. dry gin
15 ml/½ oz. Midori
30 ml/1 oz. lemon juice
20 ml/⅔ oz. simple/sugar syrup
150 ml/5 oz. sparkling
   lemonade/lemon soda

SERVES 1

Fill a balloon or 'gin tonica' glass with ice and pour in the blue Curaçao so that it sits in the bottom of the glass. Add the other ingredients (except the lemonade) to a mixing glass and stir with ice.

Gently add the mix to the glass, avoiding disturbing the Curaçao too much, then slowly pour over the sparkling lemonade. Add a straw and serve.

THANK FUNK IT'S FRIDAY

WITH BOLD ICE CUBES AND BEING LUMINESCENT UNDER UV LIGHT, THIS SURE IS A DRINK THAT YOU CAN GET DOWN TO.

50 ml/1¾ oz. dry gin
150 ml/5 oz. tonic water,
   well chilled
Disco Ice (see Note, right)

SERVES 1

Add the gin to a large glass filled with your disco ice, add your tonic of choice, stir and serve.

Note: For Disco Ice make up a 50:50 mix of colourful liqueur and water and use it to fill an ice cube tray. Midori works for green, blue Curaçao for blue and Campari for red. The flavours in the ice gradually infuse the drink as the ice melts

DISCO INFERNO

**BURN BABY BURN! THIS WARM SHARING COCKTAIL USES
A FLAMBÉ EFFECT TO GIVE A SLIGHTLY BAKED FLAVOUR. BE
CAREFUL OF THOSE EYEBROWS AND BIG, GLITTERY LASHES!**

50 ml/1¾ oz. brandy, applejack or Calvados
100 ml/3½ oz. apple juice/soft cider
4–6 dashes Tabasco sauce, to taste
30 ml/1 oz. high-proof rum
a few long strips of orange peel
orange slices, to garnish

SERVES 2

Preheat two heatproof glasses by filling them
with warm water.

Combine the ingredients (except the orange
slices) in a small saucepan and gradually heat on
medium heat for 3–5 minutes. Add the strips of
orange peel to the mix and carefully ignite the
mix using a long kitchen lighter – be careful!
Once the flame is out, pour the mix into your
preheated glasses and garnish with an orange
slice and some strips of flamed orange peel
from the mixture threaded onto picks, if liked.

Note: It is possible to make this drink in the
microwave, but the above method on the hob/
stovetop is recommended. To use a microwave,
halve the recipe, place the ingredients in a
microwave-safe glass, and heat for two separate
sessions of 30 seconds with a 10-second break
in-between (800W; adjust for your microwave).

BOURBON BOOGIE

CHOCOLATE AND COOKIES WERE POPULAR RETRO TREATS. THIS CUTE DRINK USES BOTH THE BOURBON ('BORR-BON') CHOCOLATE SANDWICH COOKIE AND BOURBON ('BURR-BON') WHISKEY. A DRINK THAT WILL TWIST YOUR TONGUE AND TANTALIZE YOUR TASTEBUDS!

chocolate sauce, to drizzle

3 Bourbon biscuits/chocolate sandwich cookies

50 ml/1¾ oz. bourbon

100 ml/3½ oz. milk of your choice
  (oat milk works well)

1 scoop vanilla ice cream

whipped cream, cocktail cherry and sprinkles,
  to garnish

SERVES 1

Drizzle the chocolate sauce inside a tall glass. Add the cookies, whiskey, milk and ice cream to a blender and blitz for 60 seconds.

Pour the contents of the blender into the glass and garnish with whipped cream, a cocktail cherry and sprinkles. Serve at once.

COOL CAT CUSTARD

Follow the same recipe as above, but use custard creams/vanilla sandwich cookies and white rum instead of the bourbon cookies and bourbon.

SOUL TRAIN

NAMED AFTER THE AMERICAN MUSICAL SHOW THAT HELPED
TO BRING SOUL, FUNK AND DISCO INTO THE NATION'S LIVING
ROOMS. THE SHOW WAS FILMED IN CHICAGO AND THE HOME
OF DISCO IS NEW YORK. THE DAILY TRAIN BETWEEN THE TWO
WAS THE 20TH CENTURY LIMITED AND THIS RECIPE IS A RIFF
ON THE 20TH CENTURY COCKTAIL.

50 ml/1¾ oz. gin
30 ml/1 oz. lemon juice
30 ml/1 oz. Lillet Blanc or
   dry vermouth
15 ml/½ oz. crème de cacao
edible gold dust/spray and
   orange zest twist, to garnish

Add the ingredients (except the gold)
to a mixing glass and stir. Strain into
a rocks glass filled with large ice
cubes. Sprinkle over the gold dust
(or use gold spray), garnish with a
twist of orange zest and serve with
a swizzle stick for additional mixing.

SERVES 1

MIDNIGHT PLANE
TO HOUSTON

ANOTHER TRANSPORT-RELATED DRINK, THIS IS
A BOURBON TAKE ON A CLASSIC AVIATION COCKTAIL.

50 ml/1¾ oz. bourbon
   (ideally a Texas bourbon such as
   Garrison Brothers or Balcones)
30 ml/1 oz. lemon juice
10 ml/⅓ oz. crème de violette
10 ml/⅓ oz. maraschino
edible gold dust/spray, to garnish

Shake the ingredients (except
the gold) vigorously with ice and
fine-strain into a tumbler containing
a single large ice cube. Sprinkle over
the gold dust (or use gold spray)
and serve with a swizzle stick for
additional mixing.

SERVES 1

LONG ISLAND ICED TEA

THIS REFRESHING AND EASY-TO-DRINK COCKTAIL DOESN'T ACTUALLY CONTAIN ANY TEA, BUT LOOKS A LOT LIKE A GLASS OF ICED TEA. IT IS A GENUINE MEDLEY OF SPIRITS AND LIQUEURS AND SHOULD BE TREATED WITH RESPECT, BUT, MADE CORRECTLY, IT IS DELICIOUS.

15 ml/$\frac{1}{2}$ oz. vodka

15 ml/$\frac{1}{2}$ oz. blanco tequila

15 ml/$\frac{1}{2}$ oz. unaged/aged rum

15 ml/$\frac{1}{2}$ oz. dry gin

15 ml/$\frac{1}{2}$ oz. triple sec

30 ml/1 oz. lemon juice

30 ml/1 oz. simple/sugar syrup

cola, to taste

citrus fruit slices and mint sprig,
 to garnish

SERVES 1

Stir the ingredients (except the cola) in a large, ice-filled glass – a pint glass works well if you have enough ice.

Top-up with chilled cola, garnish with a variety of citrus fruit slices and a mint sprig and serve.

DANCING WITH THE CAPTAIN

A DRINK THAT'S LIKE SIPPIN' ON SUNSHINE – EVEN THE CAPTAIN WOULD GET HIS GROOVE ON WITH THIS! IT'S A GOOD DRINK FOR THOSE WHO LIKE THE IDEA OF A PIÑA COLADA, BUT ARE NOT KEEN ON ITS RICH CREAMINESS.

30 ml/1 oz. dark rum
(such as Cotswolds Treacle Rum)

20 ml/³⁄₄ oz. Malibu

10 ml/¹⁄₃ oz. pineapple juice

20 ml/³⁄₄ oz. lime juice

dry roasted or salted peanuts
(see Note, below), optional

SERVES 1

Shake the ingredients vigorously with ice, fine-strain into a stemmed cocktail glass and serve.

Note: Serve this cocktail with some dry roasted or salted peanuts on the side, or better still, finely crush them and use to rim the glass!

ROCK THE BOAT

The same recipe as above, but serve in an oversized cocktail coupe and add 75 ml/2½ oz. ginger ale. The result is a longer, more refreshing drink, with a little extra bite from the bubbles. You may go all out and rim the glass with toasted coconut flakes and garnish with a pineapple wedge and lime slice, if liked.

SEASONAL

WINE COOLERS

LENGTHENING WINE AND CHILLING IT WITH ICE IS A LOVELY WAY TO ENJOY A DRINK ON A HOT SUNNY SUMMER'S AFTERNOON WITHOUT OVERDOING IT. HERE IS SOME COOL INSPIRATION.

KALIMOTXO

75 ml/2½ oz. red wine
25 ml/¾ oz. red vermouth
75 ml/2½ oz. cola
   (ideally full-sugar)
3 dashes orange bitters
orange slice, to garnish

SERVES 1

Build the ingredients in an ice-filled glass, garnish with an orange slice and serve.

PUTTIN' ON THE SPRITZ

75 ml/2½ oz. white wine
25 ml/¾ oz. pink grapefruit juice
20 ml/⅔ oz. Passoa liqueur
75 ml/2½ oz. sparkling lemonade/
   lemon soda
pink grapefruit slice, to garnish

SERVES 1

Build the ingredients in an ice-filled glass, garnish with a grapefruit slice and serve.

FLAMBOYANT FLAMINGO

75 ml/2½ oz. rosé wine
25 ml/¾ oz. bianco vermouth
25 ml/¾ oz. lime juice
25 ml/¾ oz. simple/sugar syrup
red berries and a lemon zest,
   to garnish

SERVES 1

Add the ingredients to an ice-filled blender and blitz until smooth. Pour into a glass, garnish with red berries and a lemon zest on a pick and serve.

BLUE SKIES FIZZ

A VARIATION ON THE RAMOS GIN FIZZ FOR SPRING, BUT WITHOUT ALL OF THE FUSS OF HAVING TO SHAKE IT FOR THE FULL 5 MINUTES!

45 ml/1½ oz. gin

15 ml/½ oz. lime juice

15 ml/½ oz. lemon juice

60 ml/2 oz. double/heavy cream

30 ml/1 oz. blue Curaçao, plus extra to garnish

2–3 drops orange flower water
   (this really is essential and there is no substitute)

30 ml/1 oz. egg white (or suitable substitute)

chilled sparkling/soda water, to top up

strip of lemon zest, to garnish

SERVES 1

Add the ingredients (except the egg white) to a shaker with one medium-sized ice cube (about 2-cm/¾-inch cube). Shake until the ice cube has completely melted; you'll know when this is, because it will have stopped rattling about. Add the egg white to your shaker and shake vigorously again.

Strain into a tall glass (without ice or garnish) and top-up with chilled sparkling or soda water. Garnish with a slice of lemon peel threaded onto a pick and finish with a drizzle of blue Curaçao over the top of the foam. Serve at once.

SEPTEMBER (21ST DAY OF)

HERE'S A DRINK FOR AUTUMN/FALL THAT YOU'LL BE SURE TO REMEMBER! A HOT TAKE ON BRANDY AND BUTTERSCOTCH THAT CAN BE WHIPPED UP IN A MATTER OF MINUTES. YES, PLEASE!

50 ml/1¾ oz. grape brandy

100 ml/3½ oz. butterscotch mix, hot (see below)

ground cinnamon, nutmeg or grated chocolate, to garnish

SERVES 1

Carefully combine the ingredients in a heatproof glass and stir. Garnish with a dusting of cinnamon or nutmeg or a sprinkle of finely grated chocolate, as preferred.

BUTTERSCOTCH MIX

Unwrap six Werther's Original butter candies and place in a small jug/pitcher with 100 ml/3½ oz. water. Heat on full power for 60 seconds in a microwave (800W; adjust accordingly). Stir, then heat for 60 seconds more. If you don't have a microwave, you can heat the mixture on the hob/stovetop, or use 120 ml/4 oz. boiling water and some stirring.

Variations: A dark, navy strength rum also works well with this winter warmer: the spiced, dark sugar notes complement the butterscotch of the candies. Other alternatives include: Calvados, which creates a liquid toffee apple; bourbon, which brings out a peanut-like salinity; and rye whiskey, which emphasizes the butteriness of the drink.

MURDER ON THE DANCEFLOOR

AN ADULT LEMONADE THAT WILL TAKE YOU BACK TO ALL THE FUN OF SCHOOL DANCES AND DISCOS. THE RED WINE FLOAT GIVES THE DRINK A SUITABLY SINISTER LOOK FOR A HALLOWEEN PARTY.

40 ml/1½ oz. dry gin

20 ml/⅔ oz. dry vermouth

20 ml/⅔ oz. triple sec

40 ml/1½ oz. sparkling lemonade/ lemon soda

5–10 ml/¼ –⅓ oz. red wine, to float

lime slice, to garnish

SERVES 1

Add the gin, vermouth and triple sec to an ice-filled glass and gently stir with a straw. Slowly pour the wine over the top of the ice over a barspoon so that it layers and 'floats' on the top. Garnish with a slice of lime and serve.

APRÈS SKI BOMBARDINO

PULL ON YOUR NEON SKI-SUIT AND INDULGE IN SOME HOT
DRINKS THAT WOULD HAVE KEPT YOU NICE AND TOASTY
IN A 1980S SKI LODGE.

CLASSIC BOMBARDINO

40 ml/1½ oz. hot VOV egg liqueur
or other egg liqueur, such as Advocaat
20 ml/⅔ oz. brandy
whipped cream and grated nutmeg, to serve

SERVES 1

Gently warm the egg liqueur in a pan on the
hob/stovetop (or in a bowl in the microwave
for 30 seconds). Combine the brandy and
warm liqueur in a warmed heatproof glass
and gently stir. Dollop the cream on top,
finish with a grating of nutmeg and serve.

THE CALIMERO
An alternative that replaces the brandy with
fresh espresso, giving the drink an extra kick.
Add a few sprinkles to garnish, if liked.

THE PIRATA
Substitute rum for the brandy.

THE SCOZZESE
Substitute Scotch whisky for the brandy.

THE BRITANNICO
For a fruity (no egg) alternative, warm some
sloe gin and combine it in a small preheated
cup with brandy before adding the cream.

SHERRY TRIFLE

THE CLASSIC 1970S CHRISTMAS DESSERT IN COCKTAIL FORM. THE PERFECT DRINK FOR ANY WINTER FESTIVITIES.

1 teaspoon jelly/Jello

25 ml/¾ oz. vodka

50 ml/1¾ oz. Advocaat

25 ml/¾ oz. sweet sherry

whipped cream, sprinkles and any red berries (sprayed with edible gold spray, if liked), to garnish

sponge finger (Savoiardi cookie), to serve

SERVES 1

Add a teaspoon of jelly/Jello to the bottom of the glass, then add ice. Shake the vodka, Advocaat and sherry well with ice, then strain into the glass. Top with a dollop of whipped cream, sprinkles and fruit. Serve with a sponge finger, a straw and possibly a spoon!

Note: This cocktail is rich and indulgent, with the Advocaat being a good simulation of the custard in a trifle without being too thick. The jelly/Jello adds a touch of fruitiness and the sponge finger helps you to eat the cream. A little messy, perhaps, but great festive fun!

RA-RA RASPUTIN

A VARIATION ON THE RASPUTIN COCKTAIL, WHICH IS PART
SEA BREEZE, PART COSMO, WITH THE FABULOUSLY FESTIVE
FINESSE OF FIZZ! A FINE WAY TO SEE IN THE NEW YEAR.

50 ml/1¾ oz. vodka (raspberry flavoured
    vodka works particularly well)

25 ml/¾ oz. cranberry juice

25 ml/¾ oz. pink grapefruit juice

10 ml/⅓ oz. maraschino liqueur

sparkling wine, to top up

sparkler, cocktail cherries and lemon
    or lime zest, to garnish

SERVES 1

Shake all the ingredients (except for the wine)
vigorously with ice and pour into a larger coupe
or cocktail glass. Garnish with a mini sparkler,
weighted by two cocktail cherries, and add
a thin spiral of lemon or lime zest.

Note: Be sure to carefully and safely remove
and dispose of the sparkler (once it has burnt
out) before drinking. The sparkler adds flair,
but is not integral to the taste of the drink...

INDEX

ACKNOWLEDGMENTS

The authors would like to acknowledge Sara L. Smith, without whom the book would not be possible, as well as: The Gin Archive, The Gin Genies, The Gin Guild, Stephen Kennard, Queenie & Big T, Jellybean, JPS & DWS, High Flyers 'Shak & Antonio', Team POG, Michelle & Jim Rivers, Sally & Andrew, Josh 'Muddy' Rivers, AK, Rosie the Bear & Hazza, Stupot, BP & Dr. Damo, J. Lawrie, Millie & Jersey Rich, VP, VK, EZ, Za, DAB, SG1, SEB, C-dog, The 'If I Can't Have You' Bears & Cubs, Mavis, Lorro, Lol, Allee 'Queen of Kitsch' Willis, DJ Disco Cat, Hornet Steve, TobTobs, Benny Santini, Ben & Campfire Kate, The Ausloos', Dave Smith (t'other one), Adam Smithson, Sarah Mitchell, Clayton & Ali Hartley, Bill & Erik Owen of the ADI, The New Sheridan Club, D'Eagles, Gregory Clark, The BeeGees, The Haymans, Anita and the team at Paragraph Publishing, the Spirits Business, the IWSC, Mom, Dad, Sally and Andrew, Muddy Rivers, Diamond Ken's Sister Wives, Foxzilla, Zahra, Kate Gerwin, Chanta, Carla Verenzuela, Luis Navarro, Tyler Wang, Flashdance Nance & Jason, Allie 'The Big Cheese' Klug, Kellie & Finn, BB, Sassy Chasse, Simon Brooking, Mo, Conner, Rich, Gardner, Davey Jones, Jonathan Armstrong, Edwin, Kay Quigley, Ugo, Adam Harris, Jesse Maguire, Kate McKiernan, The Donkeys, Janice Snowden, Dawn, my disco dancing partners Janice Bailon and Suzu, The Gin Girl, Benjie Lawless Watterson, Zaltfunction, Josh and the Down & Out team, The Hotsy Totsy, Joyface, Happy Accidents, Best Intentions, Tin Widow, UnderCôtê, and every nightclub bartender who had to search for that 'mine's the black one' credit card 5 minutes to close! And last but not least, my publisher Julia Charles and all the RPS team.